Keeping
Water Clean

by Helen Frost

Consulting Editor: Gail Saunders-Smith, Ph.D.

Reviewer: Carolyn M. Tucker
Water Education Specialist
California Department of Water Resources

Pebble Books

an imprint of Capstone Press
Mankato, Minnesota

Pebble Books are published by Capstone Press
151 Good Counsel Drive, P.O. Box 669, Mankato, Minnesota 56002
http://www.capstone-press.com

2 3 4 5 6 04 03 02 01 00

Library of Congress Cataloging-in-Publication Data
Frost, Helen, 1949–
    Keeping water clean/by Helen Frost.
    p. cm.—(Water)
    Includes bibliographical references and index.
    Summary: Simple text and photographs describe water pollution, how it
spreads, and its effects.
    ISBN 0-7368-0408-0
    1. Water—Pollution—Juvenile literature. [1. Water—Pollution. 2. Pollution.]
I. Title. II. Series: Frost, Helen, 1949– Water.
TD422.F76   2000
363.739′4—dc21   99-19590
                                                                              CIP

Note to Parents and Teachers

The Water series supports national science standards for
understanding the properties of water. This book describes and
illustrates ways people can keep water clean. The photographs
support early readers in understanding the text. The repetition
of words and phrases helps early readers learn new words. This
book also introduces early readers to subject-specific vocabulary
words, which are defined in the Words to Know section. Early
readers may need assistance to read some words and to use the
Table of Contents, Words to Know, Read More, Internet Sites, and
Index/Word List sections of the book.

Table of Contents

All living things need
clean water to stay alive.

Clean water keeps people, plants, and animals healthy.

Sometimes people pollute water. Polluted water can hurt people, plants, and animals.

Everyone can keep water clean. People can pick up trash from lakes, rivers, and oceans.

12

Farmers can keep water clean. They can use fertilizers that do not pollute the water.

Factory workers can keep water clean. They can keep chemicals out of the water.

City workers can keep water clean. They can clean the water that people have used.

Some groups help keep water clean. They teach people how to take care of water.

Water on the earth is always moving. Keeping water clean can help people everywhere.

Words to Know

factory—a building where products are made in large numbers; factories often use machines and chemicals to make products.

fertilizer—matter that is put on land to make the soil richer and to help crops grow; animal manure and chemical mixtures are types of fertilizers.

healthy—fit and well; clean water keeps people, plants, and animals healthy.

pollute—to make something dirty or unsafe; polluted water can hurt people, plants, and animals.

Read More

Frost, Helen. *We Need Water.* Water. Mankato, Minn.: Pebble Books, 2000.

Hooper, Meredith. *The Drop in My Drink: The Story of Water on Our Planet.* New York: Viking, 1998.

McLeish, Ewan. *Keeping Water Clean.* Protecting Our Planet. Austin, Texas: Raintree Steck-Vaughn, 1998.

Internet Sites

Give Water a Hand
http://www.uwex.edu/erc/index.html

Kids' Stuff
http://www.epa.gov/ogwdw/kids

Kid's View of a Local Water-Quality Problem
http://wwwga.usgs.gov/edu/kidsquality.html

Youth Activities Page
http://www.awwa.org/yoc-p-gi.htm

Index/Word List

Word Count: 117
Early-Intervention Level: 14

Editorial Credits
Mari C. Schuh, editor; Timothy Halldin, cover designer; Linda Clavel, illustrator;
    Kimberly Danger, photo researcher

Photo Credits
American Water Works Assocation, 18
David F. Clobes, cover, 10, 14, 16
Index Stock Imagery/Exon Photography, 8
International Stock/Steve Lucas, 4
Jack Glisson, 6
Photo Network/Paul Thompson, 1
Photri-Microstock/Fotopic, 20 (top); Lani Howe, 20 (bottom)
Wildlands Conservancy/T.L. Gettings, 12